# Marijuana
# Money

**Marijuana Money**

This handbook is an introduction to making money in marijuana businesses, including cultivation, retail sales, manufacturing edibles and infused products, payment processing, packaging, paraphernalia, testing laboratories, and paraphernalia.

# Marijuana Money

Marijuana Money

Author: Douglas Slain, M.A., J.D.

## DEDICATION

## To  Carl Sagan

"The illegality of cannabis is outrageous, an impediment to full utilization of a drug which helps produce the serenity and insight, sensitivity and fellowship so desperately needed in this increasingly mad and dangerous world."

# CONTENTS

# Chapter One: At the Beginning

As of summer of 2014 medical marijuana is legal in 20 states including New Jersey as well as Washington D.C., while two states, Colorado and Washington, have sales for recreation. Meanwhile, other states including New York, have unveiled plans to allow medical marijuana sales for the first time.

Marijuana's promise is not just in direct product sales – estimated to be a $40 billion largely underground industry – but in the launching and expansion of businesses that range from consulting to marketing to edibles to extracts to vaporizers to security devices to retail and dispensary expansions.

Some warn the industry is not ready for prime time because marijuana is still illegal under Federal law. Banks have been wary to accept deposits and institutional investors have less than keen to get involved. Further troubling is the fact that potential scams and investment bubbles are common in the marijuana penny stock markets.

Others think legalizing marijuana is simply bad public health policy. "This is big tobacco redux," said Kevin Sabet, director of the Drug Policy Institute at the University of Florida and a former Office of National Drug Control Policy official. "They know the only way to make money is to create addiction."

Still, combining capitalism with marijuana is what a majority of Americans desire. A Gallup poll showed that 58 percent of U.S. citizen's favor legalizing marijuana for recreational purposes and an even larger percentage approve of it for medical purposes.

Three *recent* events will prove seminal in the to-be-written history of the industry and finally announce a pathway for investors and entrepreneurs, sometimes now referred to "ganjapreneurs" or "cannabusinesses."

- **The U. S. Department of Justice has said it will not interfere with marijuana retail sales as long as all rules are followed and all taxes are paid.**

- **The U.S. Treasury Department's Financial Crimes Enforcement Network issued formal guidance to banks on how to do business with marijuana companies.**

- **The President of the United States compared marijuana to alcohol.**

An underground industry will finally come to the surface, or increasingly large segments of it will come to the surface.

Although there are dissenting voices. "The door is slightly ajar, but it isn't enough to let the horse gallop out," says

Jeffrey Miron, a senior fellow at the Cato Institute who favors decriminalization. While Miron believes that the marijuana industry should resemble the beer and liquor industries, he fears that marijuana's continuing Federal classification of a serious felony drug cannot be under-estimated as a problem for anyone wanting to make "legal" money.

Many investors insist they are not deterred.

"There is a whole canopy of products that goes beyond plants," Taylor West, deputy director of the 440-member National Cannabis Industry Association, says. There are cannabis-infused food and drinks, cannabis oils, and cannabis butters, to name a few among dozens of others.

Regulatory demands will spark other opportunities, such as labs to test for purity and systems to track inventory from seed to sale.

However, some marijuana investors *will* end up getting fleeced. On the less-regulated, thinly traded parts of the U.S. stock market, shares of marijuana-connected companies have been sky-rocketing. Some marijuana companies on the OTC Bulletin Board have quadrupled in value in a matter of months. Some of these companies appear to be employing the tactics of penny stock pump-and-dump schemes.

FINRA said it has seen a number of red flags among public cannabis companies, including one with a former CEO who was once indicted for a Ponzi scheme, and another publicly-held marijuana company who's CEO has served nine years in prison.

Private placements have been more solid marijuana

investments than these penny stock start-ups. See privateplacementadvisors.com and regdconsumerreport.com for more information.

## Chapter Two: A Multi-Billion Dollar Industry

A new multi- billion dollar industry became a reality when Colorado and Washington States approved recreational marijuana in late 2013. For the first time, re-sales of marijuana and marijuana extracts and edibles are legal transactions in two of the United States.

When the President of the United States publicly refers to the *relative* impact of alcohol and marijuana on our nation's social ills, as he did in early 2014, some form of Federal legalization, regulation, and taxation cannot
that far behind.

Together with a jump in the share price of publicly-held marijuana-connected companies, the private placement market for marijuana-connected businesses has exploded.

The latest volume in the Private Placement Handbook Series, PRIVATE MARIJUANA ISSUERS PUBLICLY RAISING, examines a new investment class, commonly referred to as **PIPR** and now followed on MarketWatch, that offers marijuana investors the ability to review the business plans of marijuana entrepreneurs online.

Soon there will be marijuana funding portals, now permitted under new SEC rules, offering marijuana businesses with a minimal intermediation drill and burden. For the first time, marijuana entrepreneurs will be meeting prospective investors online at a neutral forum with clear guideposts along the way.

There will no longer be a need to pay membership fees to join a group of people most of whom are actually afraid to share too much with each other anyway.

*So . . . capital is flowing in, new companies are launching, existing businesses are expanding . . . and all the while a "prohibition-premium" still obtains with cannabis-connected investments.*

**Where** are these putatively outsized, grey market opportunities?  **How** can there be any real opportunities insofar as growing, processing, and retailing marijuana all remain illegal under Federal law?

***Because, while nothing has changed in the eyes of Federal law, everything has changed in the eyes of Federal law enforcement.***

Since "the Cole Memo" (discussed below in this handbook) was released late in 2013, as long as marijuana businesses comply with *easy-to-follow Federal rules and regulations and do not violate applicable state law, these businesses have nothing to fear from the Federal prosecutors!*

Public perception of using marijuana, historically a sore point, has never been more positive, especially with the young. Sales of edibles and extracts and vaporizers, which lack the traditionally negative stigma of "smoking a joint," are booming.

Getting "high" in a healthy way has become the new fashion. Many prefer to alter their consciousness with a dried flower extract as opposed to alcohol. The next day both your friends and your body know the difference, just for starters (gratuitous editorial note).

Over twelve U.S. States are predicted to legalize some form of marijuana in the coming two or three years.

There will come a day when the Federal government will no longer classify marijuana in the same category as heroin. The inevitability of the ultimate demise of a failed war on the wrong drug is becoming more and more obvious to a majority of Americans.

Challenges remain, some serious, such as banking and taxes, and others less serious, such as regulations, moratoriums, and security. These are all real challenges but not overwhelming.

This handbook is an introduction to making money in marijuana businesses, including cultivation, retail sales, manufacturing edibles and infused products, payment processing, packaging, paraphernalia, testing laboratories, and paraphernalia.

# Chapter Three: Market Opportunities

When and if marijuana becomes legal in all 50 states, it will generate close to $50 billion in revenue, according to a growing chorus of students of the industry. To put this in perspective, the U.S. beer market annual sales are just under $100 billion, wine $32 billion annually, and coffee and tea $1.1 billion.

That $50 billion does not include black market revenue which will remain sizable no matter how many states legalize marijuana. On top of that, tens of billions of more dollars will be generated by ancillary businesses from security systems to accounting services to legal services to packaging and testing services.

There also is the burgeoning industrial hemp market, plus the edibles markets and the tincture and oils markets. Just as the consumer packaged goods industry as a whole increases as new products are introduced, the marijuana industry is now exploding with a range of product lines.

In Colorado alone for 2014 the total recreational market is estimated to be as much as $500 million. That is in addition to at least another $300 million from the medical marijuana market. *That is $800,000 in taxable income for the state and municipalities.*

Although taxes are higher with recreational marijuana than with medical marijuana, the medical marijuana market will be cannibalized in part by the recreational market. However, the aggregate Colorado market will be far larger than the former medical market. The market continues to expand significantly in a number of ways rather than just existing medical customers.

New customers include tourists and non-medical users who prefer to obey the law.

Washington's recreational retails stores will not open until mid-2014, according to press releases issued by the state. In a fully functional marketplace, annual Washington State revenue is estimated to reach $1 billion. Some knowledgeable observers estimate licensed recreational sales will amount to only 20% of the black market, largely due to taxes and state and local regulations.

Washington state has imposed an artificially low amount of space for indoor cultivation, creating a supply-side strain on the market. Also, the existing cap of only 334 licensed retail facilities may well keep the market smaller than anticipated.

California was the first state to legalize medical marijuana, in 1996. Twenty more states and the District of Columbia followed. Medical marijuana clients "medicate" and sometime actually medicate with dried flowers, edibles, plus infused and vaporized products. Treatable conditions include chronic pain, stress disorders, chemotherapy-related illnesses, and plain boredom, similar to needing a mild-beer buzz but nowhere near as harmful to your physical and mental well-being.

Recreational marijuana is sold for the same reasons most people drink beer and other spirits. That is why the beer lobby was motivated to be instrumental in defeating the marijuana initiative in 2012 in California.

Recreational users do not need licenses and do not need to claim an often spurious medical marijuana condition.

States' laws differ greatly. In general, the states with the most stable markets are the most regulated, both a curse and blessing. More and more states are moving toward greater regulation and taxation.

In 2013 medical marijuana sales were estimated at $1.4 billion in the United States. Sales of all marijuana and marijuana products was billions

## Chapter Four: The Cole Memo

Marijuana may be illegal in the eyes of the Federal government but it has recently become less illegal.

In August 2013 the U.S. Justice Department released a memorandum, written by Deputy Attorney General James M. Cole, clarifying the Federal government's approach to marijuana cultivation, distribution and sales. Known as "the Cole Memo," the document offers formal guidance to States that have legalized cannabis in some form or another.

Bottom line? The Justice Department will not pursue criminal charges against marijuana-related businesses that follow state and local regulations and comply with certain Federal guidelines.

The Cole Memo instructs prosecutors to bring marijuana-related prosecutions in only eight instances:

- Sales to minors
- Money going to criminal enterprises
- Sales across state lines

- Sales of other drugs
- Violence
- Grown on Federal land
- Driving under the influence (oddly)

**The Cole Memo, for the first time, gives marijuana businesses a clear cut frame-work of rules and regulations to follow regarding exposure to Federal prosecutors.**

*Doing business in the marijuana industry may be still be illegal, but a lot less illegal than it used to be.*

# Chapter Five: Colorado versus Washington

Which state will serve as a model for other markets when it comes to crafting a recreational cannabis regime: Colorado or Washington?

Although Washington and Colorado both legalized recreational marijuana in November of 2013, the two states have taken very different paths since then.

Colorado appears to be the obvious winner from a business perspective with its recreational marijuana market a national sensation. The industry is already generating tens of millions of dollars in sales and entrepreneurs are out-bragging each other in about huge profits.

Washington State's program, on the other hand, is has been stuck in controversy from the get-to, and it continues to experience setbacks. The latest hurdle developed when the agency overseeing the program decided to reduce the number of cultivation licenses for which a business can apply. It that were not bad enough, the agency also reduced the amount that each operation can grow. These are major changes at a late stage in the rule-making process. They will create huge problems for those who have already invested time and money in the marijuana business based on earlier assumptions.

"People are apoplectic," Washington attorney Ryan Agnew said. "Many people had already formed partnerships and made the capital outlays necessary to grow at the higher production cap."

Equally ominously, sales tax estimates released this week by another state agency were apparently based on projections that significant recreational marijuana sales might not begin until June 2015 – a full year later than originally anticipated.

This is claimed to be a worst-case scenario but that it is even being as articulated as a possibility speaks for reasons for serious concern.

Washington not only put strict limits on cultivation as well as on the number of retail stores, the original demand estimates used to set those rules now appear far too low. The state's ban on home growing in the recreational market will likely create serious supply-chain issues, giving renewed strength to the black market.

Perhaps even more significantly, there are plans being mentioned that would abandon the medical marijuana marketplace altogether, rather than create two separate markets. That is such a bad idea it is hard to take it seriously.

"The MMJ community was cut out of the drafting of (the law) and thus missed an opportunity to share their knowledge of the market and work in rules that might benefit existing MMJ businesses," attorney Agnew said. He mentioned issues with location restrictions, prohibitive tax levels and newly-determined  startup costs.

Colorado, by comparison, was careful to create a clear Separation between the medical and recreational industries. The state also gave current medical marijuana business stakeholders a real role in the rule-making process, which eased the transition.

Significantly, Colorado left the industry in the hands of the free market; there are a unlimited number of retail licenses, stores and cultivation sites. And Colorado residents can cultivate their own legally.

The fact that Colorado had a clear and strong regulatory framework already covering medical marijuana business made all the difference in the transition to recreational sales.

Washington still has not developed rules for dispensaries; hence, the medical marijuana industry as it exists is generally illegal.

Who knows? Washington's model might emerge as the operative national business model after it surmounts its initial challenges, while problems could eventually develop in Colorado if unrestrained growth invites scrutiny from Federal prosecutors.

But the early results show some hiccups in Washington's initial approach where businesses are concerned, and its move to eliminate – rather than embrace and restructure – the medical marijuana industry is a crucial mistake in the eyes of many.

For these reasons, other states considering recreational marijuana legalization will want to look at Colorado.

## Chapter Six : The Future of Recreational Marijuana

This is what you can expect in states following Colorado and Washington in the inexorable march toward legalization.

First, these states will need to have a medical marijuana initiative  ballot drive or state-wide general election to implement a program that is regulated and taxed.

Second, there will be need for the state's citizenry to become aware that the medical marijuana is a viable regulated industry with large tax bases.

Third, the state will have to pass a recreational marijuana ballot or legislation.

Fourth, the state must adopt regulations and a tax regime.

Fifth, legislation addressing packaging, seed-to-sales, and and distance regulations must be enacted and signed into law.

Finally, note that, no matter how the state goes about it, retailers and processors may well be waiting another year before opening their doors--after the laws are enacted. Of course, many ancillary services and products, such as consultants and equity crowdfunding platforms, plus marketing professionals, will be in business before any retail stores open.

Obviously, not all states believe capitalism and marijuana should have anything to do with each other, marijuana being so more pernicious than tobacco or alcohol (author jest).

Other states will over-regulate in the putative interest of the public weal. Marijuana businessmen should, if given the chance and if practicable, participate in the drafting of business-friendly laws and regulations.

Here are the key factors when looking at a state's prospects:

- **Taxation**

Washington State's recreational marijuana taxes are inappropriately high. Colorado's tax system is also under attack. There is an obvious tension going on here. Most taxes are obviously passed on to consumers. This leads to a larger share of the sales going back into the black market. Hence, lower sales and lower taxes. The same applies to regulations of course.

High taxes will have the salutary effect of proving the industry's legitimacy and attractiveness. This in turn will lead to more states enacting recreational marijuana laws. The problem, again, is that there is a healthy, established and large black market offering generally good product.

In addition to state taxes, there are municipal taxes. *Local tax revenues are a strong incentive for not implementing moratoriums.* Denver city officials are literally rubbing their hands.

Each state's pro-marijuana lobby should anticipate lobbying for local taxes in lieu of moratoriums and other restrictions of business.

- **Numbers**

Here is the rub: If a state follows the Washington business model that strictly limits both the number of retail outlets and grow locations each marijuana company (or individual) can operate, production efficiencies are dampened and chain stores are stopped in their tracks. Limiting retailers and growers to a limited number of locations may facilitate an increased number of entrepreneurs, but it strengthens the black market considerably.

- **Product**

Some states want to prohibit infused products with more than a specified amount of THC per gram. This potentially stops hash sales, as well as dabs and other oils, which are becoming more popular than smokables and are competing in popularity with edibles.

- **Non-profits**

Many medical marijuana retailers are required to be non-profits. If recreational marijuana regimes require non-profit status of retailers much available outside funding will quickly dry up.

- **Distances under the law**

In Washington State, regulations specify how Federally-mandated rules regarding distances of retail outlets from schools and other public buildings will be applied. These considerations impact commercial real estate decisions as well.

- **Seed-to-sale tracking**

Seed-to-sale security requirements track plants from the moment of propagation to the moment of sale. These requirements are meant to reassure local, state and Federal regulators that marijuana products will not re-enter the black market or go into minors' hands, cross state borders, or profit criminal enterprises.

## Chapter Seven: Top Ten Problems with Recreational Marijuana

### 1) Banking

Marijuana businesses have always had a hard time doing banking in that banks are Federally-chartered institutions. Neither checking accounts nor debit or credit accounts are permitted, in theory anyway.

However, it appears there is good news on the way. In early 2014, U.S. Attorney General Eric Holder announced that the Justice and Treasury departments were jointly working on ways for banks to work with the marijuana industry.

Furthermore, the industry actually has been using debit cards for some time, and many establishments are now accepting even credit cards.

## 2) Taxation

The big bear in the room has always been U.S. Code 280E, which reads:

"No deduction or credit shall be allowed for any amount paid or incurred during the taxable year in carrying on any trade or business if such trade or business (or the activities which comprise such trade or business) consists of trafficking in controlled substances (within the meaning of schedule I and II of the Controlled Substance Act) which is prohibited by Federal law or the law of any State in which such trade or business is conducted."

Marijuana is still a schedule I controlled substance under Federal law. The IRS/CHAMP case of 2007 provides some relieve for marijuana businesses, but see a professional.

## 3) Capital Formation

*It takes money to make money.*

Access to capital is essential for any business start-up. Until Recently most marijuana entrepreneurs relied on friends and family to fund their operations until they reached breakeven.

**Equity crowdfunding funding portals now allow start-ups and small businesses to raise money under SEC Rule 506(c in ways not possible before September 23, 2013—for the first time in over 80 years.**

**Online sites and funding portals have started to lend money to marijuana businesses and to negotiate equity investments.**

Most private investments were targeted to ancillary-only businesses prior to the Cole Memo. That is changing. Money can be found for direct investments.

No SBA loans are available.

There are several angel funds that recently entered the sector.

4) **Regulations**

Recreational marijuana is highly regulated. Paperwork and

compliance burdens should not be under-estimated and have kept many players out of the game. This reason alone may keep one in the ancillary sector.

## 5) **Local governance**

Any municipality can enact a moratorium on any marijuana business anytime it wants. Over 100 towns in Massachusetts alone passed anti-marijuana moratoriums just in 2013.

States with a track record of successfully regulated medical and recreational marijuana offer better opportunities for avoiding moratorium issues. It helps to remember that, of the twenty-one states with medical marijuana laws, only twelve allow dispensaries. The other nine states either already allow caretaker rowing and patient growing and/or are in the process of starting a dispensary system.

Here are the states with existing dispensaries:

- Arizona
- California
- Colorado
- District of Columbia
- Maine

- New Jersey
- New Mexico
- Rhode Island
- Vermont

Here are the states that have passed legislation for dispensaries but where they are not yet operating:

- Connecticut
- Delaware
- Illinois
- Massachusetts
- Nevada
- New Hampshire

Here are the states that have dispensaries operating but that are not yet recognized by the states:

- Michigan
- Montana
- Oregon
- Washington stat

## 6) Human resources

In many part of the country, "marijuana" is not a word most job candidates feature on their resume. While you can train a bud-tender in a few hours, marketing professionals and othersare not immediately eager to have a "dope" association.

Sime really good news is that this negative perception is finally and firmly changing.  There have been any number of clinical trials pointing to the health benefits of some applications of cannabis to a number of ailments, and the fast-growing edible market has far less "stoned" association.

## 7) **Prices**

Some blame high retain prices on gouging but that is not the case in many stores. Instead, prices are driven by production, competition, and taxation in that order, together with escalating rents in some cases.

## 8) **Late to the party**

Colorado is the most obvious example of this concern in mid-

2014. No one outside the licensed pool of medical marijuana dispensaries can even apply for a retail license in Colorado until October 2014, making any opening date a full year after the recreational shops started opening.

Having said that, *we really are at **the beginning of end of prohibition** of marijuana with all the opportunities that will come with it.*

## 9) The black market

The only real competition to licensed marijuana sales is the black market. One study from the state of Washington in 2013 concluded that the licensed sector of the industry will only get one in five purchasers; the others will continue to buy from their traditional sources.

Traditional or black market sources often offer convenience of delivery with hours that can be tailored to the customer. Taxes, safety, testing, seed-to-sale tracking, state-approved packaging—these are expenses of licensed outlets that the black market, traditional source does not have to pay.

Here are talking points for why a purchaser should come to a licensed retailer:

- Lab-tested quality of product
- Wide range of products
- Hard to find strains, edibles and CBD products
- Paraphernalia offered in one place
- No laws are being broken

## 10) Security

Marijuana-related crimes continue to rise due to the cash nature of the business as well as the resale-ability of the products that can be stolen. Security costs can be higher than you anticipate. Remember that is it almost never a good idea to have a gun on the premises. If you employ an armed security guard and the Federal government happens to raid your premises, you may face severe consequences.

# Chapter Eight: What is the future of specific states?

Approximately 15 states have established a path to legalizing marijuana. Some are further along than others. 2016 will be the next big year for recreational ballot measures. Meanwhile, the following obtains:

## Alaska

There is a general election vote in August 2014 that will likely approve a regulatory scheme similar to that of Colorado, plus a $50 per-ounce tax.

## Oregon

There are over 200 unregulated dispensaries in Oregon, and a need for regulation. A poll last year showed support for legalization at 57%. The legalization measure should appear on a November 2014 state ballot.

## New Hampshire

In January 2014 New Hampshire's House of Representatives voted to legalize marijuana in some capacity. The move awaits committee votes and the governor's signature.

## Rhode Island

The country's smallest state may legalize marijuana this summer. Rhode Island has already passed medical marijuana and limited decriminalization laws.

## California

55% of Californians support legalizing marijuana, but the defeat of Proposition 9 in 2012 has many proponents wishing to wait until 2016 for an expensive media push.

However, the Control, Regulate and Tax Marijuana Act, as well as two legalization initiatives, have been submitted and California could move forward as early as late 2014.

## Arizona

In December 2012 the first state-licensed dispensaries began to open after years of legal challenges. The success of the medical marijuana programs augurs well for 2016—not before; this is a conservative state.

## Maine

Maine residents are overwhelmingly in favor of legalization: 60% to 40%. Maine came close to legalizing marijuana in 2012 but industry insiders, fearing competition and taxes, undermined the efforts. Look for legalization in 2015.

## Massachusetts

Massachusetts is still rolling out a medical marijuana program that was legalized in 2012. The state will be ready for legalization in 2 to 3 years.

# Nevada

The state may be the first to recognize out-of-state cards for customers at its medical marijuana dispensaries, as implemented in 2013. The hope is for full legalization in 2015.

# Vermont

Although medical marijuana legislation was enacted in early 2014, so far only five dispensaries have opened. Strong market potential with tourists across New England.

# New York

Full legalization is several years away although there is ample support for both recreational and medicinal marijuana.

# Florida

Legalizing medical marijuana in late 2014 is possible. Aging population and tourism would lead to a healthy recreational market.

## Hawaii

Hawaii legalized medical marijuana in 2000. It has yet to legalize dispensaries.

## Delaware

Medical marijuana legalization passed in 2011. The first dispensary could open in late 2014.

# ABOUT THE AUTHOR

The author, Douglas Slain, is the managing director of Private Placement Advisors. He has worked with marijuana entrepreneurs and investors using JOBS Act solutions.

Slain has managed what is now a 1,500 member LinkedIn discussion group, "State Securities Regulation," for five years.

www.ingramcontent.com/pod-product-compliance
Lightning Source LLC
Chambersburg PA
CBHW051253170526
45165CB00004B/1690